PLANNING LDS WEDDINGS & RECEPTIONS

by

Lois F. Worlton

and

Opal D. Jasinski

Illustrated by

Lucille R. Perry

Eleventh Printing: January, 1998

International Standard Book Number:
0-88290-014-5

Horizon Publishers' Catalog and Order Number:
2005

Printed and distributed
in the United States of America by

Horizon
Publishers
& Distributors, Incorporated

Mailing Address:
P.O. Box 490
Bountiful, Utah 84011-0490

Street Address:
50 South 500 West
Bountiful, Utah 84010

Local Phone: (801) 295-9451
WATS (toll free): 1 (800) 453-0812
FAX: (801) 295-0196

Internet: www.horizonpublishers.com

Dedicated
With Love
to
Those Who Marry

ACKNOWLEDGEMENTS

We gratefully acknowledge the assistance of generous individuals and business firms in providing information and advice on weddings.

We especially thank Mr. Ezra L. Budge for continuing encouragement and for manuscript review, Mr. William J. Worlton for manuscript editing, and Mary Ann Worlton for manuscript typing.

The following individuals kindly returned questionnaires concerning wedding customs in their areas: Mrs. Arla Barney, Mrs. LaRue Cox, Mr. Duane Crowther, Mr. John Paul Fugal, Mrs. Effie Hawkins, Mrs. Carol Hirshi, Mrs. Roxie McNeil, Mrs. Faye Newville, Mrs. Keith Nielsen, Mrs. Edith O'Barr, Mr. Gerald O'Barr, Mrs. Beth Porter, Mrs. Laura Sowards, and Mrs. Bernice Haderlie.

Firms providing information on photography and catering were Z.C.M.I. Portrait Studios, Salt Lake City, Utah; Ecker's Studio, Salt Lake City, Utah; Shalamar and Crystal Room, Salt Lake City, Utah; The Reception Centre, Mollie J. Barlow, Hostess, Salt Lake City, Utah; Heritage House Reception Center and Chapel, Lenae Benson, Wedding Consultant, Salt Lake City, Utah; Tenth Ward Catering Service, Blackfoot, Idaho; Artistic Catering Service, Thomas, Idaho; For-Get-Me-Not Floral Shop, Manassa, Colorado.

Appreciation is given to Chesbros Music Co., Idaho Falls, Idaho, for information regarding appropriate music.

Helpful information was provided by The Church of Jesus Christ of Latter-day Saints Information Service, Salt Lake City, Utah, and the Los Alamos Family Council, Los Alamos, New Mexico.

For information regarding Church policies and practices we thank the following members of stake presidencies and bishoprics: I. Haven Barlow, C. Orson Cox, Roger Felt, Russell D. Glenn, and Joseph V. Porter.

Special appreciation is extended to Margaret Glad who interviews couples to be married in the Salt Lake Temple, for her careful reading of the manuscript.

TABLE OF CONTENTS

INTRODUCTION

The marriage relationship is truly universal in social history, for it is found in all known human societies, primitive and civilized, ancient and modern. This relationship is usually marked at its beginning by a ceremony or ritual and is an event of such importance in the life of man and of the community that it has been classed by anthropologists as one of the "rites of passage" which mark the passing from one stage of life to another. Rites of passage are ceremonies which celebrate the act of separation from a former status in life, the transition into a new status, and the acceptance of this status by the rest of the community. Marriage is classed with the other important events in life: birth, puberty (in some cultures), and death. These ceremonies acknowledge a change in life and give meaning to the new status. The marriage ceremony recognizes the separation from the single state, sanctions the transition to a married state, and signifies acceptance of this new status by members of the community. It is an accumulation of customs designed to impress the bride and groom with an awareness of their new roles and obligations.

The Church of Jesus Christ of Latter-day Saints teaches that marriage is more than just a rite of passage. It is a sacred covenant necessary for exaltation, so marriages are performed in the temples where they are sealed by the power of the priesthood for time and eternity. President Heber J. Grant advised

> The blessing and promises that come from beginning life together, for time and eternity, in a temple of the Lord, cannot be obtained in any other way and worthy young Latter-day Saint men and women who so begin life together find that their eternal partnership under the everlasting covenant becomes the foundation upon which are

1

built peace, happiness, virtue, love, and all of the other eternal verities of life, here and hereafter.[1]

When couples marry, this event is of importance not only to them and their families but also to their church and community. This act of marriage gives rise to the creation of a new family unit, the basic building block of society, and how well the couple manage this family has an effect on the future of the church and of the nation. With this responsibility to themselves and to society it is only wise to begin this partnership under the best possible circumstances and with the blessings of those entities which will be affected.

Because of the importance of marriage in the lives of its members the Latter-day Saint Church offers help in planning how and where they will be married. Many do not marry in the temple, so there are arrangements for Bishops and other Church officials to perform civil ceremonies. Under these conditions members are urged to have their marriage performed by their own Bishop, if possible, or by some other Church official. Every effort is made to insure that all weddings are held in the best possible surroundings and with the blessing of families, friends and church.

This booklet has been compiled to aid prospective brides and grooms in making plans which will be simple and beautiful and in keeping with the dignity and solemnity which should surround the exchange of wedding vows. It is not set forth as the "right" way to do things, but as a guide to some simple and beautiful wedding arrangements, with the hope that those who use it will have a wedding to cherish forever.

---

[1]Heber J. Grant, "Beginning Life Together," *The Improvement Era,* XXXIX (April, 1936), pp. 198-199.

PLANNING CHECKLIST

Four to Six Months Prior to the Wedding
1. Initial interview with Bishop
2. Reserve reception facilities
3. Schedule wedding ceremony
4. Schedule rehearsal, if necessary
5. Invite attendants to participate in wedding
6. Announce engagement in newspaper (optional) (four months)
7. Order or begin construction of wedding gown and attendants' gowns

Two to Four Months
1. Engage photographer
2. Engage caterer
3. Order flowers
4. Order invitations, announcements, napkins and thank you cards
5. Engage organist and soloist
6. Order cake

Six Weeks
1. Have bridal portrait taken (allows time to get glossy print processed for newspaper deadline)
2. Address invitations (Do not mail yet)
3. Purchase gifts as needed for groom, attendants and those who assist at wedding or reception or who give showers
4. Reserve rooms for out-of-town guests
5. Make appointments with hairdresser as needed

One Month
1. Get serological tests
2. Get marriage license

3. Mail invitations
4. Write thank you notes for gifts as they arrive
5. Make yourself available for bridal showers and parties
6. Arrange transportation for bridal party, if needed
7. Reserve place and make arrangements for rehearsal party or wedding breakfast
8. Double check all previous arrangements

One Week

1. Send wedding announcement with release date to newspaper
2. Purchase and prepare food
3. Decorate reception facility
4. Pack honeymoon bags

Notes

Date	*Item*

PLANNING CHECKLIST

Date   *Item*

_____   _____

_____   _____

_____   _____

_____   _____

_____   _____

_____   _____

_____   _____

_____   _____

_____   _____

_____   _____

_____   _____

_____   _____

_____   _____

_____   _____

_____   _____

_____   _____

_____   _____

_____   _____

_____   _____

_____   _____

_____   _____

_____   _____

_____   _____

_____   _____

_____   _____

_____   _____

_____   _____

_____   _____

Pre-Nuptial Parties

As the time for the wedding approaches friends begin to plan parties for the bride and groom. This is a very generous and thoughtful gesture on the part of friends and should be met by an equally generous and thoughtful attitude on the part of the bride and groom. A long series of parties is not only exhausting for the bride and groom, but can become a financial hardship on friends who are invited to several parties or showers and are expected to bring a gift to each. When too many showers are being planned, the bride should suggest that friends join with one another in hostessing such events, and friends might consult one another before planning showers to see if they can be combined. Very often the hostesses will wish to invite the same group of friends and joining forces for one or two nice showers will avoid the prospect of four or five small ones all involving the same group of guests. This will allow the hostesses to share expenses and work and allow the bride sufficient time for rest before the wedding. Few brides should allow more than two showers to be given for them.

Who Gives a Shower

The bridal shower is given by friends of the bride, or relatives such as aunts or cousins, but never by the immediate family of the bride or groom. Every guest is expected to bring a gift, so it is not in good taste for the members of the immediate families to issue such an invitation. Honor attendants to the bride or bridesmaids may give a shower, but are under no obligation to do so. Showers are often given by co-workers or business associates if the bride is employed, and can be planned during the lunch-hour or coffee-break. These informal occasions are often the most fun. It is also appropriate for friends of the bride's mother to give a shower for the bride.

Guest List and Invitations

Only close friends of the bride, her relatives, the groom's

relatives and the bridal attendants should be invited to showers. Friends from all age groups can be invited to the same shower, but no person should be expected to attend more than two showers for the bride. As a matter of courtesy and good taste the bride should be allowed to "o.k." the guest list before invitations are issued. There is the possibility that someone may be invited to the shower whose name does not appear on the reception guest list. No one should be asked to attend a shower who is not also invited to the reception. Shower invitations may be made by telephone or by written note.

Setting a Date and Time

Showers are usually given one month to two weeks before the wedding. The hostess will need to decide whether the shower will be held in the daytime or evening. Daytime showers have the advantage that they do not compete with other obligations which guests may have in the evening. Girls of the bride's own age are probably still dating and married women may have family responsibilities they can't leave in the evenings. The evening shower is more adaptable to a joint event in which the groom and his friends are invited to join the party for refreshments after the gifts have been opened. Whatever the time selected the shower should be planned to last for about two hours. Surprise showers can be fun, but are hard to arrange successfully and are not always appreciated by the recipient.

Shower Gifts

The invitation to a shower should indicate the type of gift a guest is expected to bring, such as kitchen, linen, lingerie, or miscellaneous, and should discourage the giving of expensive gifts (unless it is customary in the group).

The mother and sisters of the bride and groom are not expected to bring gifts for the bride.

It is entirely proper to give a "no gift" shower and to ask the guests to bring in the place of a gift a favorite recipe or household hint printed on a card which is placed in a file box provided by the hostess and presented to the bride.

Guests should not ordinarily be asked to contribute money toward a common gift unless it is an intimate group, such as a club, neighborhood or co-worker group.

The gifts are placed in a pile or large container as the guests arrive and are given to the bride to be opened together. This is generally the focal point of the party and often no other entertainment need be planned. This is a good time for taking candid shots with a camera provided by the hostess or brought by the bride's family.

As the gifts are opened the bride should thank each person warmly for the gift, but it is not mandatory that a thank-you note be sent. The bride should, however, send a thank-you note or small gift to her hostess.

Bachelor Parties

Bachelor parties are usually given sometime during the last two weeks before the wedding, but preferably not the night before the wedding. These can be hosted by the groom, his attendants, or everyone can go "Dutch treat." The guest list usually consists of the groom's male friends, best man, and ushers, and can include the fathers of the bride and groom. These parties often take the form of a dinner and "talk" and are an ideal time for the groom to present small gifts to his wedding attendants.

8

The Engagement

When they become engaged, most couples wish to share their excitement and happiness with friends and relatives. The question arises as to what is the best way to officially announce their intent to marry. This can be done by newspaper announcement or by a social occasion planned especially for this joyous announcement. Engagement announcements are never made by printed card.

Newspaper Announcement

When an engagement is to be announced by newspaper, the society editor should receive the account several days before it is to be printed. The release date should be clearly written across the top of the page. The announcement is made by the parents of the bride, or by her relatives or guardian in case the parents are not living. Announcement is never made by parents of the groom. The account should appear somewhat as follows: "Mr. and Mrs. William Smith, Oakland, California, announce the engagement of their daughter, Mary, to Mr. Charles J. Richards, son of Mr. and Mrs. Louis M. Richards of Seattle, Washington." The names of the schools attended by both may be mentioned, if desired. It is not necessary to specify the wedding date, but the announcement should appear three to four months before the wedding is to take place and usually no less than six weeks before. It is not a good idea for the announcement to be made as long as a year before the intended wedding.

Some newspapers will not print both engagement pictures and wedding pictures, so it will be necessary to inquire from the society editor of the newspaper about their publication policies before sending accounts in for publication. Some newspapers also ask a fee for publishing pictures accompanying engagement and wedding announcements. Before an engagement announcement is released the newspaper may call the parents of the bride for confirmation.

The Engagement Party

Engagements are often announced at a social event. This social event could be a party, buffet, dinner, dance, luncheon or whatever the couple desires, and can be as large or as intimate as personal tastes dictate. The engagement can be announced by the couple themselves, by the bride's parents or by some novel favors or decorations. The ways of announcing an engagement often depend on local custom and the bride may simply wish to announce her engagement by wearing the engagement ring.

Etiquette for the Families of the Bride and Groom

After the announcement of the engagement it is customary for the parents of the groom to call on the parents of the bride and for them to return the call within a comfortable length of time. When the two families do not know each other it is especially important for them to meet and become acquainted. If the parents live a great distance apart it is very gracious for the mother of the groom to indicate a willingness to visit the bride's parents in their home, and to suggest a time when they could be in their city and call on them. The marriage of a son or daughter ought to be of enough importance for the parents to travel a distance to meet each other. The success of a marriage often hinges on the understanding of the background of the intended bride and groom, so it is only wise that these visits are made and that both families get to know each other.

Purpose of the Engagement

The engagement is a space of time between the courtship and the marriage when the prospective bride and groom can sit back and "take stock." It is a time to review the past, evaluate the present, and take a good, hard look at the future. It allows the couple the opportunity to explore their own feelings and convictions and to become better acquainted with the character of their intended spouse. This is a time for discussing policies and attitudes which will contribute to the success of their marriage.

A good way to provoke thoughtful discussions about basic ideas of the marriage relationship is to read a good marriage manual aloud together and discuss each topic as it occurs. A good marriage manual will cover many aspects of marriage, including sex, finances, family planning, disagreements, communication and sharing of duties and responsibilities.

Wedding plans should be discussed and mutually agreed upon during this period. The wishes of both sets of parents should be solicited and considered and then a wedding planned that expresses the values of both the bride and groom. It is very easy for wedding and reception plans to get out of hand because the emotional climate is right for the bride and groom or for their parents to be manipulated by both unscrupulous and well-meaning advisors who insist that "This is the way it is done," or "This is her big moment," The temptation is great during the planning stage to engage extravagant services or to invite too many guests, some of whom are not even known to the bride and groom. Sometimes a wedding is staged for false values such as prestige, status-seeking, or business or professional pay-offs. This time of engagement allows the bride and groom to select wedding and reception procedures that will be in keeping with their real values and with the solemnity of the event, and to exclude those procedures which may be distasteful to them.

The engagement period is a good time to build relationships with the future in-laws. Many jokes are told about in-laws, but the fact of the matter is that in-laws play an important role in the success of marriages. Their goodwill and approval can be a valuable asset to a marriage and their disapproval can drive a wedge between husband and wife when a crisis develops.

11

The engagement allows time to arrange financial affairs and to get ready for the economic burden of marriage. Decisions can be made concerning the role of the wife as homemaker or as wage-earner, concerning adequate housing, and concerning the handling of money.

The engagement provides an atmosphere of security wherein couples may test the sincerity of their developing love for each other without the threat of rivals. They can see if they do indeed have common interests and compatible personalities. There is opportunity for the relationship to mature into companionship as well as romantic love, a combination which forms the best sustaining force for a satisfactory marriage.

Keeping a diary during this period of engagement and subsequent marriage is a way of remembering precious moments and happy occasions. It will be treasured in the years to come by both the bride and groom and by the children who come to bless their lives. Many happy Family Home Evenings can be spent with this book of remembrances.

The Broken Engagement

If during this period of engagement it is felt that the marriage cannot be a happy one, the engagement can be broken by either party. The engagement ring and any gifts of value should be returned. An announcement of the broken engagement may be made by newspaper, or may be circulated by mutual friends. It is not necessary to give any reason for the action. The newspaper announcement should simply say, "The engagement of Mary Smith, daughter of Mr. and Mrs. William Smith of Oakland, California, to Mr. Charles J. Richards, son of Mr. and Mrs. Louis M. Richards of Seattle, Washington, has been broken by mutual consent."

Bishop's Interview

At the earliest opportunity an interview with the Bishop should be scheduled to discuss plans for the wedding. His advice and counsel are particularly needed to make this an occasion to cherish in joyful times and to provide support in difficult times. Since the wedding day is one of the most important in a lifetime, no effort should be spared in making it memorable.

Temple Marriage

The Bishop will explain procedures and requirements and give skillful guidance in preparing for the temple marriage. Because the marriage ceremony is arranged by the temple workers it requires little planning by the bride and groom. They will need help, though, in setting a date and making arrangements for the wedding party to arrive at the proper time and place to have their marriage solemnized. The Bishop has access to information necessary for making these arrangements.

Civil Marriage

Bishops also arrange and perform civil wedding ceremonies. Couples who choose not to be married in the temple will receive the same thoughtful guidance and help as those who do. The Bishop can help make the civil wedding beautiful and meaningful with the hope that the time will come when this marriage can be sealed in the temple for time and eternity. Every couple deserves the best possible start in their new partnership and this is best accomplished in an atmosphere of love and caring.

Since the home is considered the most sacred place outside of the temple, it is suggested that civil marriages take place there. Weddings may also be held in the Relief Society Room, Cultural Hall and at the discretion of the Bishop, in the chapel. He will help the bride and groom choose the most suitable place for the ceremony. The use of commercial wedding chapels is discouraged.

There are sometimes questions as to whether particular traditional wedding procedures are appropriate in L.D.S. civil weddings. Wedding vows are more meaningful when surrounded by spirituality, order, beauty and dignity and should be planned with these criteria in mind. A good rule to follow in determining if some custom is suitable is to ask if it adds to or detracts from these four desirable qualities. If it contributes to the atmosphere of the wedding, it is probably appropriate. Traditional music has a calming effect and creates a spiritual mood; flowers add to the beauty of the surroundings; and ushers contribute to the orderly seating of guests. A wedding processional is a convenient way to get the wedding party where they belong without the appearance of confusion and disorder. The father escorting his daughter to her future husband is an eloquent expression of his approval and confidence that the groom will care for and cherish this precious daughter. When a processional or recessional is used, a rehearsal at some time prior to the wedding helps to put the bride and groom at ease concerning what will be expected of them. It allows time for small changes to be made in wedding plans, if necessary. The actual ceremony is never read at a rehearsal, but the couple will be given instructions as to their part in it. As spiritual leader of the ward, the Bishop should approve all arrangements as to place and procedure of the wedding. If there are things requested by the bride and groom which the Bishop deems unsuitable, they should graciously accept his counsel in these matters.

A simple wedding is often more beautiful and yet less costly than an elaborate one. Brides and grooms would do well to remember in their planning that they should not allow wedding preparations to become so costly as to place a financial burden on their parents or themselves. The purpose of a wedding is the exchange of vows, not the staging of an ostentatious theatrical production.

The date of the wedding should be arranged with the Bishop as early as possible to avoid conflicts in the use of church facilities. Many churches have more than one ward using them, and reservations need to be made far in advance to avoid disappointments.

There are some things which Church policy prevents Bishops from doing. They may not accept a fee for performing marriages, weddings may not take place on Sundays or at unusual hours of the night, and no candles or incense may be used at the wedding ceremony.

Planning the Temple Wedding

Because planning is the key to successful weddings it should start early and be thorough. Disappointments and confusion are avoided by careful preparation on the part of the bride and groom planning a temple wedding. There are requirements of the Church as well as legal requirements which must be met before a wedding can be performed in the temple. In addition, each temple has its own schedules, and these must be consulted before a date can be set. It is a good idea to write to the temple where the marriage will be performed to obtain requirements and schedules for wedding planning. Many of the temples provide detailed written instructions for those planning to be wed in the temple.

Obtaining a Recommend

The first step in planning is an interview with the Bishop, from whom the temple recommend is obtained. He will conduct a searching personal interview to determine individual worthiness for temple marriage. If he is assured that the individual is worthy, he will issue a recommend for marriage in the temple. This recommend must then be taken to the Stake President, who will also conduct an interview, and if his findings agree with those of the Bishop, he will sign the recommend. To be valid a recommend must be signed by both the Bishop and the Stake President. This interview will determine such things as

1. Does this person have a testimony of the gospel?
2. Does this person support local and general authorities?
3. Does this person accept and follow the teachings and programs of the Church?
4. Does this person keep the Word of Wisdom, including abstention from the improper use of drugs?
5. Is this person morally clean (free from adultery, fornication, and homosexuality, etc.)?
6. Is this person a member in good standing in the Church?
7. Is this person free from legal entanglements?
8. Does this person contribute a full tithe?

The recommend must state specifically that it is for marriage. Even if the person seeking temple marriage has a valid recommend he must still be interviewed and recommended for marriage. The recommend will not be accepted at the temple for a marriage ceremony unless so indicated on the recommend.

Couples are advised to be sure that the recommend is completely filled out on both sides by the Bishop. The recommend must show the individual's baptism date. If he has received his endowments, it must show the date he was endowed. Serious difficulties, which might even cause the marriage to have to be postponed, result if the couple arrive at the temple with incomplete recommends, for the above information is needed by temple personnel.

A recommend is not issued to anyone who has been a member of the Church for less than one year unless he has written permission from the Presidency for the sealing and endowment. This letter must be presented with the temple recommend. If a couple has had a civil marriage they must wait a year before applying for a temple recommend for sealing. The exception to this is when the couple have written permission from the First Presidency for an early sealing. The proper channel for receiving this exception is through the priesthood, beginning with the Bishop.

Though the Bishop may counsel with the couple early, he probably will not issue a temple recommend until approximately a week before the temple marriage is to take place.

Scheduling the Wedding

Because each temple has its own schedule it may be necessary to write to the temple in which the wedding will be held for a list of days on which sealings and marriages are performed. Sealings are done only on specific days and in specific sessions. When the temple is closed for vacation they sometimes set one day during the month it is closed when they will perform marriages. Some of the sessions in temples are conducted in languages other than English. It would be wise to check and see that the wedding is scheduled on a day when the proper language is spoken, so that the exchange of vows and sealing can be understood and meaningful. It could be very disappointing to be married and not understand anything that was said.

After consulting schedules, a date and hour should be set for the ceremony so that other planning can progress. It may be necessary to make travel arrangements for those living a distance from the temple and reservations should be made as soon as possible for the reception facility.

Clothing for the Temple Wedding

Special clothing is required in the temple and the Bishop has the information as to what is appropriate. If the bride or groom do not have the necessary clothing, they may rent it from the temple at the time of the wedding.

Brides may wear their wedding dress if it has a high neck (or dickey), wrist-length sleeves, and a long skirt. Since it is requested that brides do not wear trains or hoop skirts in the temple, the dress could be made so that these items are detachable.

The temples have facilities for storing the bridal dress until time for its use. They should be notified in advance that the dress will be delivered, so they may be expecting it. It will be carefully taken to the bride's dressing room and kept there until time for the bride to dress for her ceremony.

Legal Requirements

All states require a license for marriage and the license must be obtained in the state in which the marriage will take place. Since laws may change from year to year, it is wise to check the current requirements in the state in which the license is to be obtained. Most states require a serological (blood) test or a physician's medical certificate. The results from these tests may take several days and may be valid for only 30 days, so timing is important in applying for a marriage license. Some states have a waiting period after the license is obtained and couples cannot be married until the waiting period is over. This requirement can be waived by special arrangement in some states.

States have minimum-age-of-consent laws, so the couple may have to present birth certificates or written permission of parent or guardian to obtain a license. If either or both bride and groom are alien born, they will need their citizenship papers. If they are not citizens they will need passports or other proof of age, identity and citizenship. Divorced couples will have to show divorce papers in order to obtain a license and may need to obtain the license in the same county in which they are to be married.

The bride and groom should plan to go together for their license, but if this is not possible another person can obtain the license with proper authorization.

Fees for the license are small and will be one of the smallest items in the wedding budget.

Someone should be asked to be responsible for the license during the wedding to see that it is signed by the person officiating and by two witnesses, and that it is put in a safe place. If there are friends the bride and groom wish to honor, they could ask them to sign the license as witnesses.

After the wedding the license should be registered at the county clerk's office to provide legal evidence of marriage.

People have been known to neglect this important requirement and have found themselves without legal proof of marriage upon losing their marriage certificate.

The following chart notes legal requirements for marriage in the various states as of 1970. The marriage is invalid if the boy or girl falsifies his or her age.

STATE	parental consent		AGES legal		blood test required	WAITING before license issued	PERIOD after license issued
	boy	girl	boy	girl			
Alabama	14	14	18	18	yes	0	0
Alaska	16	16	18	18	no	3 days	0
Arizona	16	16	18	18	yes	0	0
Arkansas	17	16	18	18	yes	3 days	0
California	18	18	18	18	yes	0	0
Colorado	16	16	18	18	yes	0	0
Connecticut	16	16	18	18	yes	4 days	0
Delaware	18	16	18	18	no	0	24 hrs.
District of Columbia	16	16	18	18	yes	3 days	0
Florida	17	17	18	18	yes	0	0
Georgia	16	16	18	18	yes	0	0
Hawaii	16	16	18	18	yes	0	0
Idaho	16	16	18	18	no	0	0
Illinois	16	16	18	18	yes	0	24 hrs.
Indiana	17	17	18	18	yes	3 days	0
Iowa	*	*	18	18	no	3 days	0
Kansas	*	*	18	18	no	3 days	0
Kentucky	*	*	18	18	yes	3 days	0
Lousiana	18	16	18	16	yes	0	72 hrs.
Maine	16	16	18	18	no	5 days	0
Maryland	16	16	18	18	no	48 hrs.	0
Massachusetts	*	*	18	18	yes	3 days	0
Michigan	16	16	18	18	yes	3 days	0
Minnesota	16	16	18	18	no	5 days	0
Mississippi	17	15	21	21	yes	3 days	0
Missouri	15	15	18	18	no	3 days	0
Montana	15	15	18	18	yes	0	3 days
Nebraska	17	17	18	21	yes	2 days	0
Nevada	16	16	18	18	no	0	0
New Hampshire	14	13	18	18	no	3 days	0
New Jersey	16	16	18	18	yes	3 days	0
New Mexico	16	16	18	18	yes	0	0
New York	16	14	18	18	yes	0	24 hrs.
North Carolina	16	16	18	18	yes	0	0

North Dakota	16	16	18	18	yes	0	0
Ohio	18	16	18	18	yes	5 days	0
Oklahoma	16	16	18	18	yes	0	0
Oregon	17	17	18	18	yes	3 days	0
Pennsylvania	16	16	18	18	yes	3 days	0
Rhode Island	14	12	18	18	yes	0	0
South Carolina	16	14	18	18	no	24 hrs.	0
South Dakota	16	16	18	18	no	0	0
Tennessee	16	16	18	18	yes	3 days if under legal age	0
Texas	14	14	18	18	yes	0	0
Utah	14	14	18	18	no	0	0
Vermont	16	16	18	18	yes	0	5 days
Virginia	16	16	18	18	no	0	0
Washington	17	17	18	18	no	3 days	0
West Virginia	16	16	18	18	yes	3 days	0
Wisconsin	16	16	18	18	yes	5 days	0
Wyoming	16	16	19	19	yes	0	0

If under 18, parental and/or court consent required

The Wedding Budget

The wedding should be kept simple, in good taste, and in accordance with what can be comfortably afforded. The ideal plan should allow the bride and groom to enjoy and cherish the memory of the wedding. It cannot be enjoyed if burdensome debts are created or if the wedding is beyond individual means.

Bride's Expenses

Most of the expense of the wedding is borne by the bride and her parents. They pay for invitations; fees for buildings used; organist and soloist; reception costs; photographer; bride's clothes and wedding gown; hotel bills for the bridesmaids (if needed); flowers for the maid of honor and the bridesmaids; gifts for the maid of honor, bridesmaids and other attendants; a gift for the groom; the groom's ring; and gifts for those helping with the wedding or reception and for those who give showers for the bride.

Groom's Expenses

The engagement and wedding rings are purchased by the groom, although the bride and groom may wish to go together to select rings that match. The groom also pays for the marriage license; a bride's bouquet, corsages for both mothers and special relatives; boutonnieres for himself, the best man, ushers and both fathers; wedding clothes; gifts for the best man and ushers; a gift for the bride; hotel bills for the best man and ushers (if needed); and the honeymoon trip. (There are no fees charged by the Bishop or other L.D.S. Church officials for performing the wedding ceremony.)

Parents of the Groom

The groom's parents may pay for the wedding breakfast or luncheon after the temple wedding. When the wedding is a civil ceremony and requires a rehearsal, it is customary for the groom's parents to host a party or dinner following the rehearsal. These events are optional, however. They may also be hosted by the parents of the bride.

Attendants

The attendants usually pay for their own transportation, wedding outfits and presents to the bride and groom.

Reducing Wedding Expenses

The wedding expenses can be kept to a minimum with careful planning and lots of "do-it-yourself" and the wedding can still be a beautiful and dignified occasion.

The dresses for the bride and bridesmaids can be sewn by a talented bride or her mother for a considerable savings. Ready-made wedding gowns cost sixty to several thousand dollars, but the efficient seamstress can make one for much less. There are fabrics and patterns available that make lovely gowns for weddings. Fabric stores carry a wide variety of sewing notions that assist in the trimming, and some stores carry a complete line of accessories for sewing bridal gowns and veils. The disadvantage of making the bridal gown is that it may not turn out as planned. It is hard to tell if it will be exactly what is wanted until it is finished and tried on, and then it may be too late to change plans. The bride must be very careful to choose a style which will be becoming to her. Early completion of the dress is desirable as time for sewing the last few days before a wedding is very difficult to find.

Flowers for decorating can easily be seasonal flowers grown in the gardens of parents or friends. The bride will need to furnish proper containers, but she can usually find artistic friends to arrange and place the flowers just before the wedding or reception. The flowers carried or worn by the bridal party will probably have to be purchased from a professional florist because of the fragile nature of flowers. They need to be kept fresh until the time for their use.

Photographs can sometimes be an expensive item in the wedding budget. The cost can be reduced to the cost of the film and processing if a friend takes pictures of the wedding. This should be done with the realization that they may not be as well done as professional photographs.

The cost of refreshments can be lowered by buying and preparing the food without the use of a caterer. This takes considerable time and planning, but can usually be done with the help of friends and relatives. The decorating and refreshments can be prepared ahead of time. The refreshments will necessarily need to be simple and easy to serve.

Wedding Expenses

	Estimated Cost	Actual Cost
Invitations	_____	_____
Announcements	_____	_____
Reception napkins	_____	_____
Thank you notes	_____	_____
Postage	_____	_____
Total _____		
Bride's engagement and wedding rings	_____	_____
Groom's wedding ring	_____	_____
Bridal gown and accessories	_____	_____
Trousseau	_____	_____
Attendant's gowns	_____	_____
Tux rental for groom, attendants and ushers	_____	_____
Total _____		
Engagement photographs	_____	_____
Wedding photographs	_____	_____
Candid shots	_____	_____
Extra prints	_____	_____
Total _____		

PLANNING L.D.S. WEDDINGS AND RECEPTIONS

Bride's bouquet   _____   _____

Bride's attendant's bouquets   _____   _____

Corsages for mothers   _____   _____

Boutonnieres for groom, attendants and ushers   _____   _____

Flowers for wedding and/or reception decoration   _____   _____

                                            Total _____

Rehearsal dinner   _____   _____

Wedding breakfast or lunch   _____   _____

Wedding cake   _____   _____

Catering or food for reception   _____   _____

Decorations for reception   _____   _____

                                            Total _____

Music for wedding (organist, soloist)   _____   _____

Music for reception (orchestra, combo, soloist)   _____   _____

Clergy fee (if applicable)   _____   _____

Marriage license   _____   _____

Wedding site rental   _____   _____

Reception hall rental   _____   _____

Equipment rental (chairs, tables)   _____   _____

                                            Total _____

Gifts for bride's attendants   _____   _____

Gifts for groom's attendants   _____   _____

Gifts for those providing special services   _____   _____

Gifts for hosts/hostesses of parties   _____   _____

                                            Total _____

Transportation   _____   _____

Hotel Accomodations for attendants or guests   _____   _____

Honeymoon   _____   _____

Other   _____   _____

                                            Total _____

Choosing Attendants

Attendants for a wedding are chosen by the bride and groom and it is considered an honor to be invited to be part of the wedding party. These attendants are invited by the bride and groom personally, not by the bride's mother as are most guests.

Bride's Attendants

The bridal attendants are usually chosen from the bride's own family and close friends. An unmarried sister close in age to the bride is the first choice as maid of honor, and a married sister may be chosen as matron of honor. Only one honor attendant is chosen for the bride.

The duties of the honor attendant are to help the bride in every way possible. She may be a witness to sign the marriage certificate, she attends parties, helps address invitations, helps the bride dress for the wedding, helps her with her bouquet at the wedding ceremony, stands in the reception line, and helps the bride change from her wedding dress to her going away outfit after the reception. The maid of honor helps to oversee all wedding preparations and is ready to help in any way that is asked of her.

The bridesmaids may be sisters of the bride or groom, or the best friends of the bride. It is not good taste to choose a bridesmaid just to enlarge a wedding party. Bridesmaids are chosen on the basis of affection and not how their appearance will enhance the beauty of the wedding.

It is perfectly proper to decline the invitation to be an attendant, but having once accepted the invitation, the bridesmaid should drop out only for a very serious reason.

Groomsmen

The best man is selected and personally invited by the groom. Often this attendant is a best friend and near the groom's own age, but can be a relative such as a brother or the groom's father. Many young men choose to honor their own father in this way regardless of age difference.

The duty of the best man is to be a helper to the groom. He helps the groom make arrangements such as packing, reservations, and transportation for the honeymoon; he oversees the ushers, attends the rehearsal and parties, and holds the wedding ring during the ceremony. The best man could be asked to be responsible for the marriage license. He should see that it is signed by the proper people and put in a safe place for the bride and groom. If his age permits it, he is sometimes asked to sign as a witness to the marriage. The best man often does not stand in the reception line, but circulates among the guests at the reception.

Ushers are chosen from brothers, other relatives, or friends of the groom. If the wedding is small, it is not necessary to have ushers. The groom tells the ushers what their apparel should be for the wedding, supplies gloves and ties, if required, and supplies the boutonniere.

The ushers' duties are to seat guests as they arrive or to show them to their places for a home or garden wedding. The usher will offer his arm to the lady, and her escort follows behind to the place where they are to be seated. Ushers may stand as part of the wedding party during the ceremony, or if this is not desired by the groom, they stand behind the guests until the ceremony is over. Ushers usually do not stand in the reception line.

Wedding Apparel

The Bridal Outfit

The bridal gown is a very personal and important part of the wedding preparations. Great sentimental value is attached to the apparel of the bride because it is cherished in memory as the most important gown she wears in a lifetime. For this reason care should be taken in choosing a gown that enhances the natural charms of the bride. It must be becoming in style and fit. It should be the gown of her choice because on this day she wants to feel she looks her best. Even though there is an heirloom gown in the family, it may not be becoming to the bride and she should not be made to feel obligated to wear it by unthinking relatives. A gown with simple lines and few trimmings is preferable for weddings. The gown should enhance, not overpower the bride.

The degree of formality will determine the lines and fabric of the wedding dress. Formal weddings require a full-length dress with either a high or modest neckline and may have either short or full length sleeves. (The temple ceremony requires long sleeves.) Attention should be given to the appearance of the back of the dress since that is the view that guests will have during the wedding ceremony. A dress with some attractive construction features to add interest to the back is in good taste and will add to the beauty of the total picture. The dress may be just floor length or may have a short train if it does not interfere with ease of movement and if the space is adequate. The front of the dress should be at least one inch above the floor to allow the bride to walk gracefully without tripping on the dress.

The fabric should be suitable for the formality, season and surroundings of the wedding day. White is the traditional color for a bride and is a must for a temple ceremony. Pastel shade may be used for other ceremonies, if the bride prefers. The style of dress should be a factor for consideration when choosing a fabric. Satin and lace are suitable for almost any wedding gown and other traditional fabrics are tulle, brocade, moire, taffeta, velvet or velveteen, chiffon, crepe, cotton, sheer wool and some rayon and synthetics. The wedding gown is often trimmed with lace, beads or seed pearls, but trimmings should not be so elaborate that they detract from the simple lines of the gown.

The bridal veil is an integral part of the costume for the formal wedding. The length, however, is optional. It should be suited to the gown, and it can be full-length, fingertip or shoulder length. The veil usually consists of a headdress covered with lace, tulle or fabric to match the dress. The veil should be pinned on securely (with white hairpins) so that it will not slip or fall off during the ceremony or reception. Many extra hairpins give the bride a feeling of security and no worry about the headdress falling off or being pulled off accidentally.

Gloves are not usually worn by the bride because of the nuisance of removing them to put on the wedding ring. If they are worn, the left glove is removed and held by the maid of honor while the ring is put on the bride's finger.

The shoes should be of a color to match the dress. The pump with a medium heel is appropriate and should be comfortable to wear because the bride will be standing for longer than usual during the ceremony and the reception. Sandals are not appropriate footwear for a wedding.

Only severely conservative jewelry is worn by the bride. She may wish to wear pearls or other simple jewelry given her as a gift by the groom or her parents. The engagement ring can be worn, of course, but should be worn on the right hand to allow the wedding band to be placed on the left. Costume jewelry is not appropriate with a wedding gown.

Make-up for the wedding day should be applied with a light hand to avoid a harsh look. Nails should be well-groomed and if polished, a natural shade should be used. The hair should be arranged to look as lovely as possible without the use of a new or elaborate hairdo. Often a new hairdo does not turn out well and the bride looks like someone else. On this day she should look like her own beautiful self.

Either a long or short gown is appropriate for the semiformal or informal wedding. When a short dress is worn, the veil should not be longer than the dress, or a headdress of another type may be used in place of a veil. Shoes should match the dress, and jewelry should be conservative. The bride may carry a small bridal bouquet or may wear a corsage.

Bridesmaids' Apparel

The dresses worn by the bridesmaids should harmonize with the bridal gown and with each other. They should be in a color and style chosen by the bride and should match her gown in formality. The bridesmaids usually purchase their own dresses, so the considerate bride chooses something that is within the financial means of the bridesmaids or pays for the dresses herself. She also chooses dresses that are attractive to the bridesmaids in both cut and color, and suitable for future wear.

Bridesmaids are most effective when dressed alike or in harmonizing colors. Short white gloves are always in good taste and headdresses may be simple ribbon head bands, elaborate floral creations, or hats. The gloves, shoes and headdresses should be alike for all the bridesmaids. Their shoes may match or contrast the dress in color and should be a pump style because sandles are not appropriate.

At the informal wedding it is not necessary for the bridesmaids to dress alike; they should, however, wear harmonizing dresses to present a pleasing picture.

It is an expression of friendship and honor to be invited as a bridesmaid and it is the bride's prerogative to choose the costume and accessories for this occasion. If the invited bridesmaid finds that she cannot go along with the choice or lacks the financial means to comply with the bride's wishes, she should gracefully decline the invitation.

Mothers' Gowns and Accessories

Changing trends allow the mothers to dress in either long or short gowns for the formal wedding. Their gowns should be alike, however, in length. The colors of the gowns should harmonize with the wedding party, but the choice of fabric and style are dependent on what is becoming to each. The corsage presented by the groom to both mothers is chosen with care as to color and choice of flower, so it will complement the costume. When the bride's gown is short for an informal ceremony the mothers should wear short dresses also. Gloves are appropriate and hats or headdresses may be worn, if desired.

Groom

Wedding apparel for the male members of the wedding party is quite flexible, ranging from cutaways to dark business suits. The compromise most often used is the tuxedo. It is appropriate for both formal and informal wear and can be used with the black jacket for afternoon and winter weddings or with the white jacket for evening or summer weddings.

Nearly every city has a firm where formal wear can be rented. They carry in stock a complete range of sizes and make small adjustments for perfect fit. They have accessories available such as pleated-front shirts, bow ties, and studs, and are usually to be trusted for advice as to the correctness of attire for any particular type of wedding. The clothing is all cleaned and pressed between wearings. The groom will be expected to provide his own gloves (if worn), socks and shoes. The shoes should be black to match the trousers.

A dark business suit is appropriate for small informal weddings. It should be worn with a white shirt and tie.

Best Man, Ushers, Fathers

The best man, the ushers, and the fathers follow the lead of the groom in type of dress for the wedding. About one month before the wedding is to occur, the groom should write a note to each of his groomsmen in which he indicates the type of clothing to be worn. If he wishes, the groom may furnish the ties and gloves for the best man and ushers. All of the men wear a boutonniere (furnished by the groom) in their buttonholes. The boutonniere should be a single small white flower. White carnations are usually used and are worn even on white dinner jackets.

The fathers of the bride and groom wear clothing similar to that worn by the groom and both wear boutonnieres.

Military

When the groom is a member of the armed forces, the wedding apparel may be full dress uniform. Uniforms should be worn according to strict military regulations. Boutonnieres are never worn on uniforms.

Junior Bridesmaid

The dress and accessories of the junior bridesmaid should be as close as possible to the style and color of those of the other attendants but should be suitable for her age. If she is too young to wear heels and hose, she should wear ballet or strap slippers and socks to match her dress. Her headdress may be similar to the others if it is not too sophisticated for her. She may also wear short white gloves.

The Flower Girl

The flower girl may be dressed in a miniature of the bridal gown or bridesmaids dresses, or may be dressed in a very short, full and pretty little-girl's dress. Her headdress may be a simple headband or wreath of tiny flowers. The shoes should be ballet slippers in either black or white, or dyed to match her dress. She can carry either a small nosegay or a basket with flowers or rose petals in it.

Ringbearer

The ringbearer, when used, is usually young and is often dressed in a collarless dark suit with white shirt and soft tie or in an all-white suit. He may wear short trousers if he is very young. He should not be dressed as a miniature of the groom. He may or may not wear a boutonniere as personal taste dictates.

He carries the ring attached firmly to a white satin pillow.

The rings must be attached firmly because small boys have a hard time holding the pillow still and upright during the ceremony.

The Junior Usher

The young man who is a junior usher is often a teen-ager and usually does not wear the tuxedo or other formal menswear. He should wear a dark suit, white shirt, tie and boutonniere.

Invitations and Announcements

Engraved or handwritten invitations are issued for formal or large weddings and receptions. If the wedding or reception is informal a telephone call or handwritten note is sufficient. Before the guest list is made up or cards ordered, the bride must consider the available space for guests at the wedding. When the wedding is held in the temple, the space is limited and invitations are handwritten. Invitations to a wedding in the chapel or cultural hall should be limited to the number of seats available. No guest should be required to stand. In the home, garden, or Relief Society room, the guests may stand, but space should not be over crowded.

The Guest List

The mother of the bride and the mother of the groom make up the guest list and invite only family and close friends. Though a wedding or reception may be large it is not an occasion to repay social obligations. In assembling a guest list it is useful to use address books, Christmas card lists, and church membership lists. This helps to avoid the possibility of missing someone who should have been invited. A convenient way to compile and keep a guest list is to write the name, address, and other details on a 3" x 5" card and keep it in an alphabetical file box. This provides ease in addressing invitations and announcements and gives a ready reference for "regrets," recording gifts received, and sending thank you cards. This is also very useful when there are many children in a family, as the list can be easily added to or deleted from as circumstances change over the years.

Invitations

Invitations can be issued for the wedding and reception, for the wedding only, or for the reception only. When the marriage occurs in the temple an invitation is issued for the reception only, but indicates where the couple will be married. An invitation can be issued for a civil wedding ceremony and include an insert card with a reception invitation engraved on it. Invitations should be ordered in sufficient time to address and mail them no more than four weeks and no less than two weeks before the wedding.

Announcements

Many times the parents of a bride wish to announce the wedding of their daughter with no accompanying invitations. Announcements are usually sent to distant friends or relatives who would not be expected to attend a wedding or reception. Announcements may be ordered and addressed to be mailed immediately after the wedding. Weddings are never announced until after they occur.

Ordering the Invitations and Announcements

The stationer, printer, or reception center has a wide selection of invitations and announcements and can help in choosing the most suitable card for the occasion. Cards with temple imprints may be obtained. Lovely cards printed with a portrait of the bride and groom have become popular recently. The stationer has standard forms for wording an invitation and will help the bride choose the correct one for her needs. Since engraving or printing costs vary greatly, every bride should be able to find one that fits within her budget. Prices should be discussed before ordering and the stationer may ask for a deposit. This is also a good time to order any additional items such as engraved napkins, thank you cards, and informals.

Addressing Invitations and Announcements

Instructions are included with the order for the proper method of addressing invitations. They are always addressed by hand. It is suggested that the outer envelope contain the full name and address of the guest and may contain a return address, if desired. The inner envelope may either be blank or contain the names of those invited. For example, when the children of a family are invited the inner envelope may read, "Mr. and Mrs. Samuel Brown, Sarah, Stuart and James." All invitations should be mailed at the same time.

Wedding Pictures

The wedding day goes by quickly, but will be remembered for years to come through good pictures. Wedding pictures are a record of one of the most important events in a lifetime. Care should be taken in choosing a photographer, for if the pictures do not turn out well, many beautiful memories may be lost with the passing of time.

Pictures can be a major item in the wedding budget. If money is a problem, they can be taken by a talented friend. There is wisdom, however, in engaging the services of a professional photographer, if possible.

Wedding Coverage

Photographers offer coverage of the wedding day in the form of package offers. The basic item in this coverage is an album containing a certain number of color photographs of the wedding and reception. Individual photographers then add other items to their basic coverage, such as a studio portrait, glossy prints for newspapers, parent's albums and gifts, and guest books.

The photographer comes to the wedding or reception and stays until the pictures are taken that are desired in the album. In the case of temple weddings, the photographer will meet the bridal couple on the temple grounds and take pictures with the

temple in the background. Most Bishops performing civil ceremonies do not allow pictures of the ceremony itself, but pictures may be taken before and after the ceremony.

Studio portraits are usually done before the wedding.
When a glossy print is needed for newspaper accounts some studios ask for portrait sittings as much as six weeks ahead. The
advantage of having a studio portrait is that they often turn out
better than wedding-day pictures because the bride and groom
are not tired or nervous and are in a relaxed atmosphere. It also
creates a deadline to have the gown finished and the clothes for
the groom decided upon.

Scheduling

When planning the wedding day schedule, time must be
allowed for picture taking. Photographers like some time before
the reception to pose wedding parties and to get shots of the
bridal couple in different settings without interference of arriving guests. Usually about one hour is sufficient. When the reception immediately follows a civil wedding about one-half hour
should be scheduled for picture taking between the wedding and
reception. The greatest problem encountered by the photographer is the late wedding party. When appointments are made
the wedding party should be punctual in keeping them for the
most successful pictures.

Prices

Prices vary for wedding photographs according to quantity,
size, and finish, so prices should be discussed freely before the
photographer is engaged. Comparison shopping should be done
to see that the bridal pictures are what the bride and groom
wish to have for keepsakes. When the photographer is selected,
he will need to know what is wanted by the bride and groom so
he can plan his own schedule. To avoid disappointment, the
same must be done if a friend is taking the pictures. Most photographers require a deposit on the photographs.

Flowers and Decorations

Decorating

Fresh flowers enhance any wedding and may be a single eloquent blossom or a lovely floral arrangement. In choosing flowers for decorating, care should be taken to see that they complement the spiritual atmosphere rather than detract from it. The focal point of a wedding should be the area where the ceremony takes place. The proper placement of flowers will naturally bring the eye of the guest to this point. This can be accomplished with simple arrangements of suitable flowers. The flowers should be in harmony with the decor of the room where the wedding is performed, with the colors in the bridal party, and with the spirit of the occasion. Seasonal flowers or evergreens are very appropriate for weddings. Basket arrangements should be placed where they can be seen but do not obstruct the view or easy movement. Baskets or large arrangements are very easy to move and can also be part of the reception decorations. Decorations other than flowers are not in good taste for L.D.S. weddings, and candles or incense should never be used as part of the ceremony.

Bridal Party Flowers

The trend is toward simplicity in the type of flowers carried by the bridal party. The flowers may be a single blossom, a basket of flowers, or the traditional bridal bouquet. White flowers with a touch of color to blend with the colors of the wedding party are usually preferred. The flowers carried by the attendants should be all alike to present a pleasing picture. If the wedding is small or informal, the bride may choose to have corsages for both herself and her attendants.

The boutonniere is worn by the men in the wedding party and by other special guests such as fathers and grandfathers of the bride and groom. The exception to this is when military uniforms are worn. Flowers are never worn on a military uniform.

The mother of the bride and the mother of the groom wear corsages that complement their costumes and should be chosen with the same care as for any formal occasion. Grandmothers should be remembered with a corsage when they are present at the wedding.

Lovely and interesting effects can be created by using fresh flowers in place of icing flowers on the wedding cake. These are placed just before the reception to prevent wilting.

Using Garden Flowers

As a convenience for the bride's family, the arrangement of the flowers may be performed by others. It can be done by friends or by a professional florist. Because of the fragile nature of cut flowers, they must be arranged and put in place very shortly before the ceremony and the members of the wedding party will be busy with other arrangements at the time when the flowers need to be taken care of.

The expense will be considerably less if the flowers can be cut from seasonal gardens and arranged and placed by friends. The hazards of this kind of arrangement are the uncertain blooming periods and fickle seasonal weather. The kind of flowers planned may be unavailable from local gardens at the time they are needed.

Florist Services

The professional florist is well equipped to handle all arrangements concerning flowers for weddings. He has the necessary equipment to keep cut flowers fresh until they are used and his professional pride demands that flowers be delivered on time and in perfect condition. A wilted bridal bouquet is very poor advertising for a florist.

To aid in the selection of bouquets, boutonnieres, corsages, and arrangements, the florist has samples, catalogues, and price lists. He can advise as to the kinds of flowers available and can suggest which would be most suitable. The florist can help make the best selection of flowers for the money budgeted for this item. Simplicity and beauty should be adhered to as the objectives in making the selection.

Wedding Music

Wedding Music

As the flowers at the wedding add beauty for the eye, the music adds beauty for the ear, sets the mood, calms the nerves and creates a peaceful feeling for something beautiful—the wedding ceremony.

The musical numbers should be chosen and the people asked to perform them well in advance of the wedding, since it often takes many hours of practice to perfect the music for weddings. The organist can suggest appropriate numbers or can give guidance as to whether a favorite song would be more suitable as part of the wedding music or should be performed during the reception. Certain types of music may detract from the dignity and solemnity of the marriage ceremony. The organist is generally qualified to assist in making decisions concerning the appropriateness of the music. Generally, classical and sacred numbers can be used for both the wedding and the reception. Popular love songs should be reserved for the reception only.

The organist plays for about twenty minutes before the bride enters, creating a peaceful spiritual setting as the guests arrive for the ceremony. It is sometimes necessary, when a wedding is delayed, for the organist to play indefinitely. It is wise for the organist to have sufficient music prepared to cope with this emergency.

The vocal soloist or instrumental soloist (guitars and horns are not appropriate) performs one or two numbers just after the bride's mother is seated and just before the wedding march and the entry of the wedding party. The choice of musical numbers should be appropriate to the occasion (no Ave Marias), using the bride's requests if possible.

A fee should be offered to the musicians performing for weddings and receptions. If the fee is declined it is appropriate to present them with a gift of appreciation for their efforts.

Reception Music

Soft background music adds a great deal to the atmosphere at a reception. It can be piped in from records or tapes or can be live music in the form of combos, organists or other instrumentalists. Care should be taken that the music doesn't become so loud that it drowns out attempts at conversation.

Music for receptions is handled in several ways, depending on the wishes of the bride and groom and, to some extent, on local custom. Some receptions have background music only. In some areas a program is held at some specified time in the evening and has a master of ceremonies and usually four or five musical, dance, or humorous monologue numbers. Other bridal receptions have soloists or groups providing musical numbers at intervals during the reception. When there is dancing at the reception, an orchestra or combo is hired to provide the music.

Some music that is suitable for organ and for soloists as part of the wedding ceremony or reception follows:

Organ Collections

Title	Publisher
Classical Wedding Music for the Organ	Lorenz
Easy Wedding Music for the Amateur Organist No. 2	Lorenz
Ethel Smith Wedding Music	C. Hansen
Standard Wedding Music for the Organ	Lorenz
Wedding Music for Organ	O. Ditson
Wedding Prayers to Music	Cosmopolitan
What Now My Love & Other Great Love Songs	Harms
With My Love	Big 3
32 Wedding Songs: Solos for Voice, Piano or Organ	Remick

WEDDING MUSIC

Organ Music

Title	Composer	Publisher
Bridal Chorus (Lohengrin)	Wagner	G. Schirmer & J. Fischer
Largo	Handel	G. Schirmer
Wedding Carillon	A. Schreiner	J. Fischer
Wedding March (A Midsummer Night's Dream)	Mendelssohn	G. Schirmer & Marks
Wedding Prelude	A. Schreiner	J. Fischer

Solo Music

Title	Composer	Publisher
A Time For Us (Romeo and Juliet)	Rota	C. Hansen
All The Things You Are	Jerome Kern	T. Harms
Always	Berlin	I. Berlin
An Affair to Remember	Warren	Feist
April Love	Webster - Fain	Feist
Because	D' Hardelot	Chappell
Calm as the Night	Carl Bohm	G. Schirmer & K. Fischer
I Love You Truly	Jacobs - Bond	Boston
I Married an Angel	Rogers	Robbins
If I Could Tell You	Idabelle Firestone	G. Schirmer
If You Were the Only Girl	Ayer	Remick
Ich Liebe Dich (I Love Thee)	Grieg	G. Schirmer
Just For Today	Seaver	S. Fox
Lara's Theme (Somewhere My Love)	Jarre	Robbins
O Perfect Love	Burleigh	Presser
Oh, Promise Me	De Koven	Robbins
Sunrise, Sunset	Bock	Valando
The Girl That I Marry	Berlin	I. Berlin
The Lord's Prayer	Malotti	G. Schirmer
The Prayer Perfect	Speaks	G. Schirmer
The Sunshine of Your Smile	Ray	Harms
Theme From Love Story	Sigman - Lai	Hansen
True Love	Porter	Chappell
Turn Around	Reynolds, Greene, Belefonte	Clara

What Are You Doing the Rest of Your Life?	Legrand	Big 3
With a Song in My Heart	Rogers	Harms
Why Do I Love You?	Kern	Harms
You Are Love (Showboat)	Kern	Harms
You're Nobody Till Somebody Loves You	Morgan - Stock - Cavanaugh	Southern
Yours	Roig	Marks

The Temple Wedding

Temple weddings are carefully supervised by workers at the temple who do everything possible to make the wedding a sacred and memorable event. The workers remain close to the bride and groom after they enter the temple to help them feel at ease and to assist them in any manner necessary. Because of their assistance and guidance, there is no need for wedding rehearsals or similar activities. Details are explained to the couple when they enter the temple and as preparations for the wedding are being made.

Guests

The bride and groom may invite guests, but should keep their lists limited to families and those who are very close friends. No guest may come who does not have a current temple recommend. Guests should be invited by a handwritten invitation about two weeks before the wedding and should be advised as to the time they should arrive and what clothing will be needed for the ceremony.

It is very important for the bride to determine the time guests should arrive at the temple, because if they are late they may not be able to attend the wedding ceremony.

Most temples require that guests dress in temple clothing even if they do not go through the sessions, and all temples have

43

clothing for rent that is suitable for use by anyone in the wedding party. In some temples the sealing rooms are located in such a place that guests may witness the marriage in street clothes, providing they are modest. Men may come with long-sleeved white shirts and jackets. Women should be appropriately dressed—no mini-skirts, slacks or pant-suits. Attire should be appropriate to the intimate and spiritual nature of the event.

Endowment and Sealing

The bride and groom must have their endowments before they can be sealed in marriage. There are three ways this can be handled: (1) the couple may receive their endowments and be sealed in marriage the same day; (2) they may go through the endowment session at some time prior to the wedding day and have their marriage performed on a "scheduled" basis, which means that they attend only the wedding ceremony on the wedding day; or (3) they may receive their endowments prior to the wedding day and also elect to attend the endowment session as well as the sealing ceremony on the wedding day.

Many couples prefer to have their endowments and sealing the same day, particularly when they must travel a long distance to come to the temple. Ample time should be allowed for the first-time endowment and the marriage ceremony. The wedding party will need to arrive 30 to 45 minutes early and it takes three and one-half to four hours to complete both ceremonies.

The "scheduled" ceremony is much shorter since the bride and groom do not attend an endowment session on the wedding day. The sealing takes about 20 minutes and the wedding party is asked to arrive about one-half hour before the scheduled time. It is necessary to make arrangements well ahead of time with the temple for the "scheduled" wedding.

Any of the above arrangements are suitable and should be determined by each individual couple according to their tastes and available time. When a reception is planned for the same day as the temple marriage it should not be scheduled too close to the wedding, since sessions sometimes take longer than planned.

Who May Perform the Ceremony

Each temple has people ordained to officiate at weddings—

the presidency of the temples and other workers assigned as sealers. Couples being married are requested to use the assigned officiators unless they know one of the officiators personally; then they may request that he perform their ceremony. Many times couples would like to ask one of the general authorities to perform their wedding, but in view of their tremendous work load, this is often impossible, so couples are discouraged from asking these brethren unless they are relatives or personal friends.

When a Couple Must Travel Overnight

If the prospective bride and groom live a long distance from the temple the travel will often involve overnight accommodations. When this is the case, it is advised that the bride and groom do not travel to the temple together, but with their respective families.

Miscellaneous Rules

Since cameras are not permitted inside the temple, arrangements should be made with the photographer to meet the bride and groom for pictures outside the temple. The bride may wear her wedding dress for these pictures or she may change to her street clothes. The photographer may wait in the temple foyer at the appointed time or he can be called after the ceremony and allowed time to arrive for the picture-taking.

The temple presidencies have requested that no rice or confetti be thrown on the temple grounds and that horn-honking or the use of other noise-makers be dispensed with near the temples.

When Parents Cannot Attend the Temple Wedding

There are cases where the parents of the bride or groom are unable to enter the temple to see their children married. The First Presidency and the Council of Twelve have issued a statement concerning this:

> Frequently couples whose parents, one or more, are not members of the church desire to be married by civil ceremony before going to the temples so that the non-member parents may witness the marriage. It is contrary to policy to grant such requests. In lieu thereof, if the parties concerned desire to do so, they

may arrange through the bishop of the bride or groom for the holding of a meeting in the cultural hall or some room other than the chapel subsequent or prior to the temple marriage which the nonmember parents and other friends may be invited to attend. This meeting might include a musical number, such as a vocal selection, and prayer, and the bishop of the ward or some other qualified person might explain to those present the principle of eternal marriage. There would, however, be no exchanging of vows or marriage ceremony of any kind as a part of this arrangement.

Under no circumstances may a civil marriage ceremony follow a temple marriage. This would be mockery and something that cannot be condoned.[2]

If the parents are not to attend the ceremony they may drive with the wedding party to the temple and wait on the temple grounds or in the temple foyer.

The Wedding Breakfast or Luncheon

Following the temple marriage a luncheon or breakfast may be given. This can be hosted by either the groom's parents or the bride's parents. All those who are in the wedding party should be invited, whether they attended the temple ceremony or not. Parents and close relatives should receive an invitation to this luncheon.

The luncheon could be held at a restaurant, a hotel, or at home. If held someplace other than the home, reservations must be made stating the approximate time and the number of persons expected to attend.

There are caterers who specialize in the wedding breakfast or luncheon. They could be engaged for this occasion and all arrangements left to them.

If these events are held in the home, food could be prepared the day before and heated and served to the guests after the wedding, or friends could have the meal ready for the wedding party when they arrive from the temple.

---

[2]"In Case Your Parents Can't Enter the Temple to See You Married...: Policies and Procedures," *The New Era*, I (January, 1971), p. 30.

The Home Wedding

A very dignified and meaningful ceremony can be held in the home. Many people prefer to take this all-important step in familiar and loved surroundings with those people as guests who are most important to them. Of course, the size of the home puts natural limitations on the guest list and usually only relatives or very close friends are invited.

Physical Arrangements

There are various arrangements that can be used to accommodate the wedding and guests even in small homes. A focal point should be chosen for the ceremony. This could be in front of a picture window, a fireplace, draperies, a bank of flowers, or any place that allows room for the wedding party to stand for the ceremony. Allowance should be made for the guests, too. It is permissible for the guests either to sit or to stand, depending on the room available. If the guests are to be seated, chairs should be arranged on two sides of the room with an aisle between them for the bride and other members of the wedding party to enter. If the guests are to stand, the parents and friends of the bride should stand to the left and the parents and friends of the groom should stand to the right. Space should be left for the wedding party to enter and take its place at the spot where the marriage is to occur.

Dressing Rooms

Arrangements should be made for a room somewhere in the house to be used as a dressing room for the bride, another for the use of the groom and his attendants, another for the bridesmaids. (If there are not a sufficient number of rooms, bridesmaids may arrive already dressed or a dressing room may be arranged at a close neighbor's house.) It is nice for a room to be set aside for the use of the father of the bride where he can be alone or relax before the wedding takes place.

Greeting Guests

Because the mother of the bride will probably wish to be with her daughter before the wedding, arrangements should be made for someone to greet the guests and to show them where to sit or where to stand until time for the ceremony. This greeter could be a relative or close friend, or, if the wedding is to be very formal or catered, someone could be provided by the caterer to perform this duty. When a wedding is informal the mother of the bride may wish to do this herself.

The Wedding Ceremony

A few minutes before the ceremony is to begin the groom's parents take their place to the right and the entrance of the mother of the bride is a signal that the ceremony is imminent. The mother of the bride is the last one to walk down the aisle or to enter before the wedding party and she is seated or stands to the left.

If a prayer is to be offered by someone other than the Bishop it could be done at this point. If the prayer is offered by the Bishop he usually does so just prior to the reading of the ceremony.

The solos or musical numbers are performed after the mother of the bride has been seated and before the wedding party enters.

The groom, Bishop, and best man take their places next.

When the wedding party is ready, the signal is given to the organist and the processional begins. If seated, the guests should stand as the bride enters. The bridesmaids, and then the flower girl, precede the bride and her father down the aisle. They should walk at a slow pace and about eight steps apart. Do not use the hesitation step—it makes most people appear awkward. A smooth, even step is most dignified and graceful for the occasion. The bride walks down the aisle on the right arm of her father. He leads her to a spot directly in front of the Bishop and then steps back. The groom steps to his left and takes his place at the side of the bride. The Bishop then inquires, "Who gives this woman in marriage?" The father answers, "I do," or "Her Mother and I do." He then sits or stands next to his wife. If pertinent, the Bishop asks the guests to be seated. The bride hands her bouquet to her maid of honor or bridesmaid, and the Bishop performs the marriage vows. Usually the exchange of vows is prefaced by a short sermonette or advice concerning the joys and responsibilities of marriage.

When the ceremony is over, the bride and groom may walk down the aisle together if they wish, or they may simply turn to receive congratulations from family and friends. If the reception line is to form at the point of the marriage, the parents of the bride and groom should take their places beside the bride and groom to greet guests.

If a reception is to be held immediately following the wedding in another part of the house, the bride and groom and parents should go to that spot and form a receiving line. This spot could be a foyer, a patio, garden, lawn, or any place where there is sufficient room for the guests to pass freely along the receiving line and then pause to chat or move around, if desired. Transportation will need to be provided if the reception is to be held at some other place immediately following the wedding ceremony.

Processional

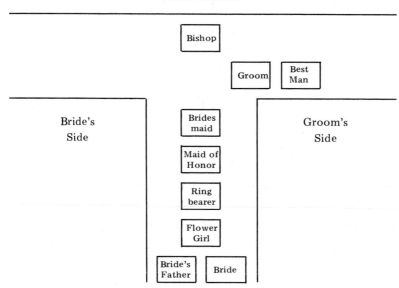

Ceremony

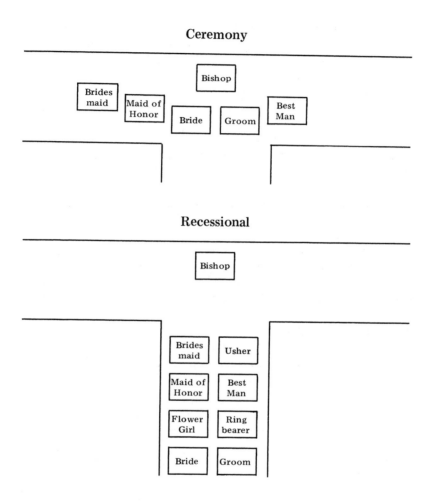

Recessional

Weddings With No Traditional Arrangements

Sometimes people wish to do away with any traditional procedures at all. In this case the wedding is performed much like the Justice of Peace wedding. The participants and witnesses simply take their places before the Bishop and he performs the marriage vows.

Garden Weddings and Rehearsals

A garden is an especially lovely place for a wedding when the flowers are in bloom. A bank of blooming flowers, a lovely tree, or any favorite spot makes an excellent background for a wedding ceremony. The arrangements are similar to those of the home wedding. Chairs can be set up on the grass, or guests may stand for the ceremony. When the wedding is planned for the garden, there must be arrangements made in case of inclement weather. It should be possible to move the wedding indoors or to have the area where the ceremony is to occur covered by a canopy. Many receptions are also held in the garden when the wedding occurs in a warm season.

Many weddings are held in Relief Society rooms and the arrangements there follow those of the home wedding very closely.

The Rehearsal

For a wedding to go smoothly and without confusion it is necessary to have a rehearsal. There may be exceptions to this, and when there are, a conference should be held with all those taking part in the ceremony so that they will know exactly what is expected of them as their part of the proceedings. A wedding day is difficult enough without the uncertainty and embarrassment of mistakes. A rehearsal allows time for making small changes in procedures and one should expect that some changes will be made.

Who Should Attend Rehearsals

All those who are taking part in the wedding are expected to attend the rehearsal. This would include the bride and groom and their parents, the Bishop, organist, soloist, best man, ushers, bridesmaids, and ringbearer and flower girl, if used. It is a good idea to have someone who will act as wedding director at the rehearsal and ceremony to give cues and to remind the participants of what they are to do. This will take pressure off the bride and her mother to see that things go right, because sometimes cues are missed in the excitement of the day.

Procedures

It is expected that during a previous interview with the Bishop, the bride and her parents have already agreed on the procedures to be followed for the ceremony. There may be some things that the bride desires to be done that are against the wishes of the Bishop. Since he is the final authority on matters concerning weddings, his wishes should be graciously adhered to.

All procedures should be walked through. The organist will need to coordinate the music with the processional and the principals need the confidence provided by going through the procedures at least once or twice. The wedding vows are not read at rehearsals, but the Bishop will give the bride and groom instructions as to their responses. If something is forgotten at the ceremony, the Bishop will be very helpful in giving quiet instructions.

Ushers' Instructions

At some time during the rehearsal the ushers should be given instructions concerning the seating of relatives and special guests of the bride and the groom. Space is reserved near the front for these guests and it is the ushers' responsibility to see that the right people are seated in this section.

Rehearsal Dinner

Sometimes a rehearsal dinner is given as part of the wedding festivities. This takes place after the rehearsal and all the participants are invited. Grandparents should be invited even though they take no active part in the ceremony. Other close family members or friends may also be invited. This dinner is usually hosted and paid for by the parents of the groom, but may be appropriately done by the parents of the bride.

Weddings in the Chapel or Cultural Hall

The cultural hall and, under some circumstances, the chapel may be used for weddings. Both of these provide more room than the home and can accommodate large wedding parties and many guests. It is important to remember in using either of these places that the guest list must be limited by the amount of seating available. No guest should be expected to stand for the ceremony.

Physical Arrangements

When the wedding occurs in the cultural hall, chairs should be set up so that there is a center aisle for the bride and her attendants. The focal point of the ceremony should be designated in some obvious way, such as with floral arrangements or an appropriate backdrop. When flowers are used they should be placed so that they do not obstruct the view or prevent easy movement.

Arrangements will need to be made to have appropriate musical instruments on hand. Quite often an organ is not available to the cultural hall without having one brought in. A piano may be used for the wedding music, but the organ is more effective.

Rooms in the church may be set aside for the use of the bride. She and her bridesmaids might use the Relief Society room, while other classrooms might be assigned for use by the groom and his attendants. When the church is used for dressing, it will be necessary to bring mirrors and set them up beforehand. Other items to aid in dressing should be brought, too. Some of these things are hair pins (white to match the veil), needle and thread, scissors, extra hose, combs, tissue paper, smelling salts, and safety pins. If it is more convenient, the bride and the wedding party may dress at home and only arrive at the church in time for the ceremony. When this is done it is necessary to provide transportation for everyone in the wedding party so that they will all arrive at the same time. There is the risk that the wedding clothes will be wrinkled or crushed with this type of arrangement. The arrival time should be scheduled quite carefully so that the wedding party does not arrive too early or too late.

The wedding should always start at the time indicated on the invitation.

The organist should begin playing appropriate music about twenty minutes before the ceremony is scheduled to begin. The guests should arrive early and be seated in their places at least five minutes before the announced time of the wedding. Guests should wait to be seated by an usher. He will inquire, or the guest may indicate, whether the guest wishes to be seated on the bride's side or the groom's side. Ladies will take the usher's arm and the gentlemen should follow slightly behind as they are shown to their seats.

As the time for the ceremony is imminent, the parents of the groom are ushered in and seated to the right and the mother of the bride is the last person to be seated by the ushers before the ceremony begins.

If a prayer is to be offered by some person other than the Bishop, it should be done at this time. When the Bishop offers a prayer, it is usually done at the beginning of the ceremony. The solo or musical number is performed before the entry of the wedding party.

In some chapels or cultural halls there is no side door or side aisles through which the Bishop, groom and best man can enter. In this case, they walk down the aisle and take their places at the front where the ceremony will take place and await the wedding procession.

When the wedding party is ready the organist is signaled and begins to play the wedding march. The guests stand for the bride. If ushers participate in the ceremony, they are first to walk down the aisle and usually walk in pairs. They are followed by the bridesmaids who may walk singly or in pairs. The maid of honor follows the bridesmaids and if there is a ringbearer he comes next. The flower girl walks in front of the bride or may walk with the ringbearer. As previously noted, the hesitation step is not used as it makes most people appear awkward. A smooth even step in time to the music makes a very graceful and dignified procession. About eight paces should be kept between each person or couple in the procession. As they reach the end of the aisle, the ushers take their places to the right and the bridesmaids take their places to the left, leaving enough room for the bride and groom to stand in the center.

The bride takes her father's right arm. He should be careful to give her enough room that her dress and veil do not catch on the seats as they pass by. The bride and her father walk directly to the front and stop before the Bishop. The father steps back and the groom takes his place to the right of the bride. The Bishop may ask, "Who gives this woman in marriage?" The father responds, "I do," or "Her mother and I do." The Bishop asks the guests to be seated. The father seats himself by his wife. The bride hands her bouquet to the maid of honor and the ceremony begins. Wedding rings are exchanged at the conclusion of the ceremony, or as instructed by the Bishop. The maid of honor and best man have usually been entrusted with the rings. If there is a ringbearer, he has both rings on a satin pillow. The groom places the bride's ring on her finger. If it is a double ring ceremony, the bride then places the groom's ring on his hand. The groom may then kiss the bride.

At the end of the ceremony the bride and groom turn and face their guests and walk back down the aisle together as the organist starts the music for the recessional. They should not run, but may walk more quickly than for the processional. They are followed by the rest of the wedding party in the reverse sequence they used in the processional, except the best man may escort the maid of honor out and the ushers may escort the bridesmaids out. The ushers then come in and usher the guests out row by row, beginning with the mother and father of the bride, then the mother and father of the groom.

When the reception immediately follows the wedding, some time (usually about one-half hour) should be allowed for picture-taking and for the wedding party to form the reception line before the guests proceed to the cultural hall or the place of reception.

Chapels With Two Main Aisles

Many chapels are built with two main aisles and seating space on both sides of the aisles. This arrangement requires special planning if there is to be a processional and recessional by the wedding party.

The processional could go down the right aisle, which has the advantage of leaving the wedding party in their proper places when they all arrive at the point of the ceremony. They could have the recessional down the left aisle. The family and guests could be seated in the center section only with the bride's side to the right and the groom's side to the left, which is the reverse of the traditional seating arrangement. If more room is needed, guests could sit in sections to the right and left of the center section.

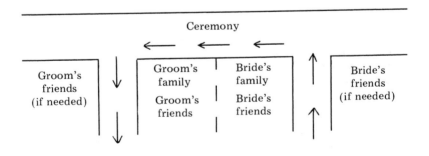

The seating would also be appropriate with the parents and friends of the bride in the extreme left section and the parents and friends of the groom in the extreme right section and friends of both seated in the center section.

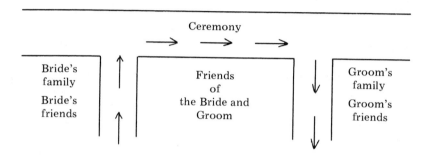

Another alternative is to use only one half of the church and have the other half blocked off. The wedding party would then use the same aisle for the processional and the recessional and the guests would be seated immediately to the left and right of this aisle. When this arrangement is used the ceremony takes place immediately in front of the aisle that is used.

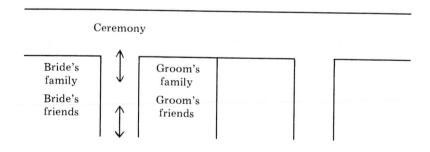

Newspaper Announcement of the Wedding

The parents of the bride announce the wedding after it takes place. This can be done both by printed cards and by an article in the society section of a local newspaper. The newspaper announcement usually contains an account of the wedding and a picture of the bride or the bride and groom together. Some photographers furnish glossy prints for newspaper announcements as part of the wedding package. Some newspapers charge a small fee to cover the cost of engraving the picture. The account of the wedding with the release date written on it and the glossy print stapled to it (to avoid loss on the editor's desk) should be delivered to the society editor of the newspaper one week before the wedding. It is wise to check with the newspaper again just before the wedding to make sure the article will be printed at the desired time.

The account of the wedding should contain such details as: the principals; the officiator; a description of the bridal gown, veil and bridal bouquet; a description of the bridal attendants' attire; an account of the schools, careers and clubs of the bride and groom; mention of any distinguished relatives; and the new "at home" address. Some newspapers will ask for such items as out-of-town guests and decorating details.

The Reception

The reception is a happy occasion and usually a gala affair which allows the guests the opportunity to offer good wishes and congratulations to the bride and groom. When the groom and his parents (or the bride and her parents on some occasions) are from another city, the reception offers them the opportunity to meet guests with whom they are not acquainted.

While the wedding ceremony is limited by custom, solemnity, and form, the reception has no such restrictions. It can be planned with the degree of formality the bride and groom wish. Receptions take many forms, depending on the circumstances, local customs, and finances of the couple, and seem to be limited only by the imagination.

Scheduling

The reception is usually held the afternoon or evening following the wedding ceremony, although in some areas they are being held a week or so after the wedding. This, of course, is an individual choice and often depends on whether the bride and groom are married in their own home town. In the case of temple weddings where the bride and groom and their families must travel a long distance to arrive home, the reception cannot possibly be held the same day as the wedding. It should be scheduled at the convenience of the bride and groom and their parents. When pictures are to be taken at the reception the bride should schedule one-half hour to one hour for the photographer prior to the start of the reception and then see that the wedding party arrives punctually. The complaint expressed most often by photographers and wedding consultants is the late arrival of the wedding party.

Decorating

Church cultural halls may be used for wedding receptions and most receptions are held there. The church offers both familiar surroundings and enough space to accommodate many guests. The cultural hall may be decorated following traditional wedding themes or any other theme which is suitable to the dignity of the occasion. It should reflect the simplicity and beauty surrounding the joyous event.

Decorations often consist of a simple backdrop for the receiving line with baskets of flowers at each end. The refreshment table can be elegant with the use of the wedding cake, the punch bowl, flower arrangements, and crystal and silver serving pieces. Small tables should be set up for the comfort of the guests and can be decorated with small floral arrangements or favors. When small tables are used there should be enough seating space for about one-third to one-half of the expected guests. The table which holds the guest book is often decorated with an arrangement of flowers, the guest book, and a pen for use by the guests in signing their names. There should be a gift table covered with a cloth or paper if gifts are to be displayed.

Themes other than traditional wedding themes are sometimes used for receptions. For instance, a young couple with ranching backgrounds used a western theme for their reception. The bride wore her traditional wedding dress and the groom his dark suit, white shirt and tie, but all the attendants were in western dress. The bridal attendants wore long calico dresses and the groomsmen wore western shirts and cowboy boots. The decorations were western and refreshments were served from tables covered with red and white checkered cloths.

Cake Cutting

Before the receiving line forms, the bride and groom cut the wedding cake. The first piece should be cut from the lower tier with a knife that is decorated with tiny fresh or artificial flowers. The groom places his hand over the bride's on the knife and they cut the cake together. The first slice is for the bride and groom and from this they feed each other one bite, the bride eating first. The cake cutting is then finished by the person serving the refreshments.

The Receiving Line

The receiving line should form at a spot where guests may move freely along to offer their greetings and then have room to pause or move around or visit before going on to the refreshment table or to be seated for serving. The sequence of the receiving line is a matter of choice; there seems to be no universally agreed-upon arrangement. It seems to work out best, though, for the mother of the bride to stand first in the line since she is the hostess, and next to her the father of the groom. This arrangement assures that everyone who comes down the line will probably be known to either the mother of the bride or the father of the groom and can be greeted and introduced by name to the other. Next in line will be the mother of the groom and then the father of the bride. Standing by her father will be the bride and at her side the groom. The maid of honor and the bridesmaids in that order make up the rest of the receiving line. Ushers and best man usually do not stand in the line, but circulate among the guests. It is optional for the fathers to stand in the receiving line; if they prefer they may circulate among the guests to see that everyone is happy and enjoying himself.

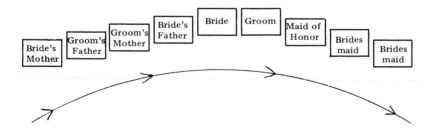

As the guests move down the receiving line they may comment on the beauty of the wedding or the gowns and offer their best wishes to the bride and their congratulations to the groom. The bride is never congratulated. Visiting in the receiving line is to be discouraged, particularly when there are a great many guests who wish to offer their best wishes to the bride and groom.

If young bridesmaids or flower girls are used in the line, arrangements should be made for them to stand for only short periods. An exhausted six-year-old does not add much to a receiving line. Some couples with small sisters have found that having the young girls take turns in a line is a good solution.

Throwing the Bouquet

Before leaving the reception it is the custom in some areas for the bride to throw her bouquet to her bridesmaids. The tradition is that whoever catches it will be the next bride. The bride may deliberately throw it to her unmarried sister or friend, or she may throw it over her shoulder to the bridesmaids. If the bouquet is the type that has a corsage in it, the corsage should be removed before it is thrown. The bride may also choose not to throw her bouquet, but to save it and give it to some special person who may not have been able to attend the wedding and reception.

Going Away

After the bouquet is thrown, the bride and groom retire to their dressing rooms to change into their going-away clothes. The maid of honor accompanies the bride and helps her with her clothing. The maid of honor has charge of the wedding dress and sees that it is delivered safely to the bride's home. When the bride and groom are both ready, the parents are informed and they come to say their good-byes. As the newlyweds leave the reception and get outside the guests may throw rice or confetti. Some ward buildings have rules against this practice and the guests must be advised of these rules. Rice or confetti should never be thrown inside a building. Following the departure of the bride and groom the guests leave the reception.

Heckling

It is the custom in some areas to decorate the car of the newlyweds and to tie old shoes and tin cans on the back bumper, or to engage in other forms of heckling. This can add to the gaiety of a wedding, but sometimes tricks of this nature are carried too far and cause unhappiness or embarrassment to the newly married couple. Occasionally the results of heckling the bride and groom have proved disastrous. It would be well for the groom to consider locking the car up in the garage of a trusted friend or member of the family and using another car until his own is used for the honeymoon. True friends help to make the wedding day one to be remembered with joy.

Thank Yous

After they leave the reception and have arrived at their destination, it is an expression of consideration for the bride and groom to call the bride's parents and thank them for the reception and other wedding arrangements. A call to the parents of the groom is also a very thoughtful and appreciated gesture.

Open House By the Groom's Parents

When the groom's family and friends live a great distance from the bride's home the parents of the groom may wish to hold an open house for the bride and groom. This is done after the reception and may have a wedding theme, if desired. Punch and cake may be served, but the cake should not be a decorated-tiered wedding cake. That is appropriate only at the bride's reception. An open house is a nice gesture on the part of the groom's parents because it gives the bride an opportunity to meet relatives and friends of the groom who could not attend the reception, and it gives friends the opportunity to extend their best wishes to the bride and groom.

Refreshments

The refreshments served for a reception range from a festive punch and wedding cake to complete meals, depending on the time of day the reception is held and the type of reception.

Most frequently, cake, punch, candy, and nuts are served. Service is usually buffet style from an elegantly-decorated table, or guests may be served at small, simply decorated tables.

The traditional tiered wedding cake, punch bowl, crystal, silver, and flower arrangements make a lovely refreshment table, pleasing to the eye and providing ease in serving guests. Napkins engraved with the names of the bride and groom are a pleasing addition to the refreshment table. This table should be placed far enough away from the reception line to allow people enough space to pause and chat or to move around after passing through the reception line.

It may be desirable to have friends of the family assist with the refreshments for the reception. There is often a kind friend who will manage the food preparation and serving for the bride. Many times younger friends of the bride are eager to act as waiters and waitresses during the reception. Care should be taken though, not to ask someone to do this who would rather come to the reception as a guest. When friends are assisting, it is better to hire help to work in the kitchen. It is sometimes an imposition to ask guests to wash dishes when they would rather be enjoying the reception.

Wedding cakes should be ordered well ahead of the wedding, and punch ingredients and other foods should be assembled in ample time for ease in preparation. Arrangements should be made for people to help with the serving and clean-up, and equipment should be in readiness well before the reception is to take place. The small tables for serving could be set up and decorated by those who are decorating the reception room.

It is difficult to estimate the number of people who will attend a reception. An accepted way of doing this is to request a reply (R.S.V.P.) on the invitation and to take the list of acceptances and add to that one-fourth to one-third of the number who did not respond to the invitation.

The reception punch bowl could be filled with one of the following punches which have been served successfully at wedding receptions. Each recipe makes 100 servings.

RECIPES FOR PUNCH

Wedding Punch

2 46-oz. cans unsweetened pineapple juice
4 12-oz. cans frozen pink lemonade concentrate
2 12-oz. cans limeade concentrate
6 12-oz. cans water
4 qt. lemon-lime carbonated beverage

Mix juices and chill. Just before serving, pour over ice. Add water and carbonated water. Yield: 100 servings.

Golden Glow Punch

4 3-oz. packages orange-flavored gelatin
4 6-oz. cans frozen pineapple-orange juice concentrate
16 cups apple juice
4 1-pint, 12-oz. bottles (14 cups) ginger ale, chilled

Dissolve gelatin in 1 cup boiling water. Stir in pineapple-orange concentrate. Add apple juice and 3 cups cold water. Carefully pour in chilled ginger ale. Makes 100 servings.

Red Wedding Punch

12 C. cranberry juice
4½ C. sugar
9 C. pineapple juice
6 C. orange juice
6 qt. ginger ale
Raspberry sherbet

Combine first four ingredients; fill a ring mold with mixture. Freeze for ice. When ready to serve, pour ginger ale and sherbet into bowl. Float ice ring in punch. Yield: 100 servings.

Gifts

Gift giving and receiving are a traditional part of marriage. From earliest times the exchange of gifts has been part of the marriage ceremony and probably is related to the concept of the dowry. In each society and era there have been certain rules which pertain to the giving and receiving of gifts. Ours is no exception.

Acknowledging Gifts

Probably the most important of these rules (and one of the most abused by brides) is the acknowledgement of gifts received. This abuse is sometimes a result of carelessness and sometimes a result of negligence. Great care should be taken to acknowledge gifts promptly.

Thank-you letters for gifts received are the responsibility of the bride and they should be handwritten. The note should mention the gift and should include a few words of appreciation of a personal nature. All gifts should be acknowledged as soon as they are received because people are entitled to know that their gift arrived. Sometimes, when many gifts are arriving immediately before or on the day of the wedding, it may not be possible to write notes the day they arrive. In this case the notes may be delayed a few weeks, but never more than three or four months after the wedding. People who have been gracious and thoughtful enough to select and send a gift deserve a prompt thank you.

In cities, gifts for the bride are most often delivered to her home in advance of the wedding. A good way to see that all gifts are acknowledged is to buy a gift-listing book from any stationery, department or book store. These books will often be sold as marriage books with space for guests' signatures, gift-listing, photographs and memory pages. There are several published now for temple weddings. It will have pages for listing gifts and donors and have numbered gummed stickers to be placed on the gifts. As each gift arrives it should have a number placed on it securely (sometimes the glue doesn't adhere too well), and it should be listed as to name of donor, what the gift is, the store in which it was purchased, the date received and the date acknowledged.

In rural areas, gifts are often brought to the reception, opened, and displayed there. When this is done, *some responsible person should be in charge of this operation.* The gifts must be unwrapped, numbered, and recorded before being set out for display. Great care must be taken to record the gifts, donors and numbers correctly. When handling a great many gifts at one time it is easy to make mistakes. As the gifts are displayed it is a good thing to avoid placing a very expensive gift next to an inexpensive one. Cards received with the gifts are usually not displayed with the gifts, but are put aside for the bride and groom.

Displaying Gifts

The question of displaying gifts is one that must be decided on an individual basis. More and more often now the gifts are left wrapped when they are delivered at the reception and are unwrapped at a later time by the bride and groom. In times past, it has been an inflexible rule that if any gifts are displayed, all gifts must be displayed, including those received at the home prior to the wedding. A recent trend in some areas, however, is to display gifts received before the reception, but to leave wrapped gifts which arrive at the reception.

When the wedding or reception is held in the home the wedding gifts should be displayed, perhaps in a room set aside for this purpose. They can be arranged on tables covered with white cloths and placed around the walls of the room. The tables need to be sturdy enough to hold the weight of the gifts placed on them. It is not in good taste to display the bride's trousseau, but her linens may be displayed.

It is the custom at some receptions to have children take the gifts from guests when they arrive and deliver them to the people who are unwrapping and displaying them. Someone should be on hand to supervise these children and to see that the gifts are handled with care. Sometimes children, in their excitement, become careless or forgetful about where the gifts are placed. A guest who has spent time, money and effort to select a gift for the bride does not like to see it handled improperly or damaged before it is given to the bride.

If a wedding is cancelled all gifts must be returned to their donors. In the case of postponement the gifts may be kept.

Catering

Many brides prefer to have a caterer take care of all or part of the reception arrangements. Catering services offer as much or as little help as is wanted by the bride and her parents. Their charges are usually made on an itemized basis. Catering services range from the large commercial chapel and reception centers to the woman down the street who likes to do catering as a hobby.

The advantages of hiring a caterer are many. They are experienced in managing receptions, have the necessary equipment, and can furnish the required people for serving, preparing food and cleaning up. All of these things relieve the bride and her family of many small, worrisome details that are very time-consuming.

Reception Centers

The chapel and reception centers provide such services as bridal-consulting, invitations, napkins, full catering, flowers for room decoration, cake knife and quill pen for the bride book. Some centers have their own photographers and provide the guest and gift books. Background music or combos can be provided by the centers and the piano and organ are available for the use of entertainers invited by the bride. They have room for dancing, if desired as part of the reception. Personal flowers for the bridal party are usually not provided by the reception centers.

These centers were designed to be used for receptions and the decor enhances the beauty of wedding parties. The prices are on an itemized basis and the bride may choose the services she wants. The refreshments are priced on a per-person or per-hundred-persons basis. The reception center must be reserved early; some specify six to eight months during the busy months (June, August, and September) and some request four to five months for reservations. On occasion the reception centers have handled arrangements on two weeks notice, but the bride must be willing to compromise on dates and times on such short notice. A deposit is usually required to reserve the reception-center facilities.

Other Catering Services

In many areas there are groups or individuals who offer catering services. For example, there is a catering service in Blackfoot, Idaho, that provides services for receptions and then donates their profits to the ward budget. They most often cater for receptions held in cultural halls and offer complete decorating of the hall, kitchen help that evening, and complete clean-up after the reception. The decorating includes a backdrop, floral arrangements at the ends of the backdrop, serving tables, tablecloths and centerpieces, guest-book table, gift tables (these are covered in matching lace, as is the cake table), and additional hall decorations as needed—topiary trees, garden scenes, sparkle boards and fountains. They provide the guest pen, silver cake-knife, serving dishes, punch and mints, and the necessary equipment for serving and clean-up. The only things the bride is responsible for are the guest book, the cake, napkins, and the flowers for the bridal party.

In Manassa, Colorado, a lady runs a catering service for local receptions. The bride's mother suggests the menu and the food is prepared to order. The bride pays for all the food, plates, cups, napkins, forks, and flowers for the arranging. The caterer then charges a nominal flat fee for her services which include decorating a bride's table, refreshment table and gift table, preparing and serving the refreshments, and cleaning up after the reception. She furnishes all the tablecloths, punch bowl, candleholders, and candles, and arranges a floral centerpiece.

There are caterers who only prepare the food and the decorating; serving and clean-up are done by the bride's family or friends.

In almost every community there is someone, either a professional caterer or someone who likes to help with weddings as a hobby, who can be engaged to help with the wedding reception. The range of services is unlimited and the bride is sure to find catering services to fit her particular needs.

The Honeymoon

The groom is responsible for making arrangements for the honeymoon. Although some grooms surprise their brides, it is usually wise for her to participate in the planning.

It is not necessary, nor sometimes even desirable, to plan a glamorous or lengthy honeymoon trip. Many young couples make plans that are far too elaborate for their financial means and thus start their marriage in debt. Some couples plan to travel too far on the honeymoon and find themselves so hurried and exhausted that they cannot enjoy the trip or each other. Both of these mistakes defeat the purpose of the honeymoon. The honeymoon should provide the newly married couple with an interlude when they may be together without ordinary day-to-day worries. Where they go is not so important as the fact that they do go and be by themselves. A honeymoon is not the time to visit relatives no matter what the pressures.

Conclusion

Wedding arrangements have a way of continuing for some time after the wedding. There is the wedding gown to be cleaned and stored away, those late wedding gifts to be acknowledged, some gifts to be exchanged, or packed away for future use and, of course, setting up housekeeping in a new apartment or house. Usually in the rush of the wedding there is not time to fill in all the pages of the wedding book, and this is a good time to finish the record of that momentous day.

The wedding day marks the beginning of a new way of life and no matter how lovely and perfect that day is, it is only the first of many more wonderful days to come. The wish of the authors to those who use this book is very aptly expressed in the wish of a mission president to a former missionary on the occasion of his marriage, "May the Lord bless you both, that your love for each other might increase with the years and that as you reach the sunset in life you can say that it is as glorious as the sunrise."[3]

---

[3]Letter, Albert Choules, President, Southern States Mission, to William J. Worlton.

SUGGESTED READINGS

After the excitement of the wedding, the time comes when the couple has to settle down to the business of learning to live together and of making their marriage happy and successful. This marriage relationship will literally be a creation of their own making. To help with this on-going process of successful marriage, many people who are knowledgeable in the field of marital counseling have written books of advice. These books cover various aspects of marriage and have proved helpful to young (and old) couples in achieving and maintaining successful marriages.

There are many readily-available sources of reading material on marriage and its problems. The public library will have a good general section on this subject. For specific information on finances, banks, credit unions, and other financial institutions are good places to go. The Department of Agriculture provides help in homemaking through Extensive Service County Home Agents located in almost every county.

Following is a list of books by both L.D.S. and non-L.D.S. authors that may be helpful to couples contemplating marriage and to those already married.

General Counseling:

All These Things Shall Give Thee Experience, by Neal A. Maxwell, Deseret Book Co., Salt Lake City, Utah, 1979.

The Art of Loving, by Erich Fromm, Harper and Row, New York, 1956.

Conjoint Family Therapy, by Virginia Satir, Science and Behavior Books, Palo Alto, Calif., 1982.

Couples, by Carlfred Broderick, Simon and Schuster, 1979.

Enriching Your Marriage—A Tune-Up for Partners in Love, by Dr. Clark Swain, Horizon Publishers & Distributors, Inc., 1982.

How to Make Your Child a Winner: Ten Keys to Rearing Successful Children, by Victor Cline, Walker and Company, New York, 1980.

Man's Search for Meaning, by Victor Frankl, Washington Square Press, New York, 1984.

Miracle of Forgiveness, by Spencer W. Kimball, Bookcraft Publishers, Salt Lake City, Utah, 1969.

People Making, by Virginia Satir, Science and Behavior Books, Palo Alto, Calif., 1972.

The Quest for Love and Self-Esteem—New Insights from Psychology and Religion, by Virginia Bourgeous, 1976.

Spiritual Roots of Human Relations, by Stephen R. Covey, Deseret Book Co., Salt Lake City, Utah, 1970.

Talking Together: Couple Communication I, (and cassette), by Sherod Miller, Elam Nunnally, Daniel B. Wackman, Interpersonal Communication Programs, Inc. Minneapolis, Minn., 1979.

That's Not What I Meant! by Deborah Tannen, William Morrow and Co., Inc., 1986.

Financial Counseling:

Money Dynamics For The New Economy, by Venita VanCaspel, Simon and Schuster, New York, 1986.

Rich on Any Income, by James P. Christensen and Clint Combs, Shadow Mountain, Salt Lake City, Utah, 1985.

Home Management:

The American Medical Association Family Medical Guide, by Jeffrey R. M. Kunz, Random House, New York, 1982.

The Aerobics Program for Total Well-being, by Kenneth H. Cooper, Bantam Books, New York, 1982.

Confessions of an Organized Housewife, by Deniece Schofield, Writer's Digest Books, Cincinnati, Ohio 1982.

Is There Life After Housework? by Don Aslett, Writer's Digest Books, Cincinnati, Ohio, 1985.

Wedding Etiquette:

The Amy Vanderbilt Complete Book of Etiquette, by Letitia Baldridge, Doubleday and Co., Garden City, N.Y., 1978.

How To Get Married and Survive It—A Guide to Wedding, Reception and Honeymoon Planning, by Beth L. Hilton, Horizon Publishers & Distributors, Inc., 1980.

Miss Manners Guide to Excruciatingly Correct Behavior, by Judith Martin, Warner Book, New York, 1982.